GARGOYLES AND GROTESQUES

GARGOYLES AND GROTESQUES

Paganism in the Medieval Church

Ronald Sheridan and Anne Ross

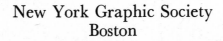

New York Graphic Society
Boston

International Standard Book Number: 0-8212-0644-3
Library of Congress Catalog Card Number: 74-21494

Designed and produced in England by London Editions Ltd, 30 Uxbridge Road, London W12 8ND
First published in 1975 in the United States by New York Graphic Society Ltd, 11 Beacon Street, Boston, Massachusetts 02108

Printed in England

Preceding page
The 'Green Man', a painted roof boss in Canterbury Cathedral

Contents

Preface

What are these fantastic monsters doing in the cloisters under the very eyes of the brothers as they read? . . . What is the meaning of these unclean monkeys, these savage lions, and monstrous creatures? To what purpose are here placed these creatures, half-beast half-man, or these spotted tigers? I see several bodies with one head and several heads with one body. Here is a quadruped with a serpent's head, there a fish with a quadruped's head, there again an animal half-horse, half-goat. . . . Surely if we do not blush for such absurdities we should at least regret what we have spent on them.

So wrote St Bernard of Clairvaux* in the twelfth century concerning the grotesque decoration of the Christian churches which were at that very time being built all around him in France and Western Europe. St Bernard's question was plainly rhetorical since, if he really wanted to know, he had but to ask the first stonemason of the many he would find at work in his own church. That he objected violently to the inclusion of grotesque art in churches is clear: that he knew but would not admit the real reasons for it is implied in his saying, '. . . if we do *not* blush for such absurdities. . .', thereby giving us a clue both to the reasons for this strange church decoration and the attitude to it of the religious hierarchy in medieval times.

Today we see medieval churches by the thousand spread throughout the length and breadth of Europe in which an enormous and uncounted number of grotesque representations are to be found, which, as St Bernard rightly points out, must have cost a great deal of money to make. Since grotesque carving is by no means essential to and is in fact almost antipathetic to the aesthetics of Romanesque or Gothic architecture, there must have been very powerful reasons for its inclusion. The generally suggested reason is that these figures represent Satan and devils from Hell. This explanation is seen not to apply to most of the grotesque figures after only a cursory

Opposite
Column capital at Schwäbisch
Gmünd, Germany

*St Bernard of Clairvaux, *Apologia ad Guilb. Sancti Theodorici abbat.*, ch. xi. *Patrol.*, clxxxii., col. 916

7

examination. Again, if this really was the reason, surely St Bernard would have known it too and said so?

The real explanation, which is preferred in this book, is that medieval grotesque art stems directly from earlier pagan beliefs, that the representations are pagan deities dear to the people which the Church was unable to eradicate and therefore allowed to subsist side-by-side with the objects of Christian orthodoxy. A modern example of this situation is to be seen in parts of South America where church imagery still includes much that is pagan belonging to the period before the Spanish conquest. The people's religion can still only be described as part-Christian, part-pagan.

As has been said, medieval grotesques and gargoyles exist by the thousands and to catalogue them all would be a major undertaking requiring not one but many volumes far weightier than this. What can be done here, however, is to break what almost seems to have been a conspiracy of silence by introducing just a few of the commonest grotesque figures, showing something of their origins where these can be traced and pointing to probable sources where they are known or can be deduced.

There are no contemporary documents, or almost none, to which we can turn for information. The evidence is in the objects themselves, and the constant repetition of similar themes during centuries of church building in every country in Europe surely constitutes a major document in itself. Evidence of certain pagan themes is to be found in objects known to be pre-Christian such as certain Celtic archaeological finds, and those from Classical Greece or the Roman Empire. Some of these are illustrated for the sake of comparison, and to assist the reader are also dated. The rest of the illustrations are all of medieval Romanesque or Gothic origin and, since it is of no especial concern to the purposes of this book whether they be of the eleventh or fourteenth century, have not been dated.

Many of the carvings reproduced here are to be found half lost to sight high up on the ceilings of the naves of great cathedrals and can only be brought into view with the aid of very powerful telescopic lenses; others are hidden in the gloom of unlighted crypts and chapels requiring long and patient searching. Most have been taken from inside the buildings since there they are found perfectly preserved whereas those outside, if they are still original carvings, are often so weatherbeaten as to make them unrecognizable. Those which have been 'restored' in recent times are worthless; for this reason some of the best-known grotesques such as those from the Cathedral of Notre-Dame de Paris have not been included. As far as is known, only original unrestored unbowdlerized medieval material is here presented.

Finally, a definition of 'grotesque' should be given. A grotesque object, for the purposes of this book, is taken to be one representing something abnormal or normally impossible such as a Centaur, half-horse half-man. A merely ugly representation does not come within the scope of this book, nor does naïve work where the artist's ability was perhaps limited. Only in those cases where a grotesque representation exists, in which the artist plainly knew exactly what he intended, has inclusion been made.

Introduction

The poet Herrick records for us, in verse, an impressive spell for exorcism:

Holy Water come and bring:
Cast in salt, for seasoning:
Set the brush for sprinkling.
Bring ye sacred spittle hither
Meale and it now mix togeither.
And a little oyle to either.

Give the tapers here their light:
Ring the saints-bell to affright
Far from hence the evill sprite.

Here we have all the ingredients required by Christianity in order to rid it of the constant and powerful forces of evil which ever lay in wait for the devout soul—in the church, in home, in the fields, on water, herding beasts on hill and moorland. *Water*, sanctified by the priest, or drawn in ritual fashion from some holy spring or well; *salt*, symbolic of eternity and spiritual preservation; *spittle*, used on the eyes, ears and nose of an infant immediately after birth, symbolic of Christ and of the vital life-fluid of the body; *meal* and *oil*, ancient ingredients of libation and propitiation; *tapers*, used to light the holy candles; the pealing of the *bells*, which in themselves have a complex and ancient lore stretching right back into the mists of the pagan past. This verse gives us an accurate and impressive idea of the folklore and belief which underlies so much of the ritual of our churches in Britain and the rest of Europe—ritual whose presence is remarkable and whose origins are often elusive or indeterminable.

The folklore of the Church is complex and vast. The aspect which concerns us here is the enormous repertoire of pagan or seemingly pagan imagery which largely finds expression in the great variety of grotesques and gargoyles which adorn the Gothic churches of the West and continue into the ensuing periods. Apart from studying the style and distribution of these strange objects, we must consider their symbolism. Are we to regard them as actual pagan *survivals* which a tolerant church has permitted its members to incorporate in the structure for superstitious reasons? Were they used as symbols of evil and the fate lying irrevocably ahead for all sinners, a warning to the erring to return to the paths of righteousness before it was too late? The church was very much a place of instruction in medieval times, and to a largely illiterate congregation its message must of necessity be conveyed with the assistance of symbols, or picture-writing. By selecting imagery which was familiar to the people the church could the more easily convey its message.

Although there are innumerable variations on the basic themes, there is also throughout Europe a remarkable, fundamental consistency which makes it quite clear that whatever their *raison d'être* their presence in the sacred buildings was not random but deliberate. In some examples, the horrific and sometimes frankly crude features are deliberately emphasized, the repulsive characteristics made immediately obvious. In other cases, the first impression may be innocuous; only close study may suddenly reveal a sinister and sometimes positively frightening aspect, which is all the more impressive because it is so subtly concealed beneath a bland, almost naturalistic façade. The astonishing frequency and widespread nature of these grotesque features in the European Church is indeed noteworthy.

It has often been suggested that when they are placed on the outside of the sacred building their presence symbolizes the evil forces which lie beyond the sanctity of the structure itself; once past them, safety was assured. This argument cannot, however, really be supported. Many of the most horrific, seemingly pagan and frankly sensual subjects are found in the interiors of churches. Some are tucked away in obscure corners, where it takes a very skilful photographer to record them. But others are blatant and obvious, and their presence must have been acceptable to the authorities.

If we are unable, from our present-day perspective, and on account of the lack of documentary evidence, to comprehend the exact significance of this great corpus of grotesque imagery in the Gothic Church, we can at least make some attempt to understand the sources from which it ultimately derived, and to isolate elements which seem to go back to genuine pagan contexts from those which appear to be purely fantastic, the creation and foible of some individual craftsman. Many of the themes we have selected could, and most probably do, have a variety of different sources and traditions, which have amalgamated and moulded them to the particular form in which we find them. Where indigenous traditions of the pre-Christian period could comfortably find parallels with Christian dogma, it would be possible to weld the two together so that, like the Bicorporates themselves, the two bodies could be joined by a single head representing the two streams of tradition unified by the final form of the grotesque. So latent superstition would be satisfied, and the old beliefs utilized to make intelligible the teaching of the Church.

Before we can consider the pagan survivals in these features we must glance at the background of Europe in pre-Christian times, in order to detect any themes or motifs which were widespread and deeply-rooted enough to make it likely that their survival would be lengthy. European prehistory is at present in a state of flux. Opinions and ideas are changing as knowledge increases, and a re-thinking of the past is becoming increasingly urgent. This affects the iconography of the later, Christian, world in various ways. It is now appearing to be more and more evident that the coming of the Iron Age to Europe north of the Alps by about 650 BC was rather a technological revolution than an ethnic change. In other words, the people here who were affected by the Iron Age were not newcomers, but the indigenous bronze-using populations who, it is becoming ever more demonstrable, were Celts of some kind, most probably speaking some form of Celtic or proto-Celtic language. We find an astonishing longevity of and consistency in religious motif and concept. Symbolism, which is highly developed in the early historical period, and which is explicable either by inscription or by classical commentaries, can be shown to have a direct ancestry stretching well back into the middle of the second millennium BC, and probably much further. Motifs dating to the beginning of that millenium find a convincing echo in Gothic iconography, and many cult ideas have a continuity which, no matter what new influences were brought to bear on the actual symbolism, derive their origins from Europe's most remote past.

At the height of its power, between 500 and 300 BC, the Celtic world stretched from the Black Sea to the Atlantic Ocean, from the Baltic Sea to the Mediterranean. The oral memory was intensively cultivated, with the result that the entire rich religious tradition was deeply embedded in the minds of the people. Underneath all the strife and change entailed first by the coming of Rome and subsequently by the descent of the barbarians on Dark Age Europe, by the change resulting from the spread of learning and ideas from the east, and by all the heterogeneous influences of the early Christian Church, a constant stream of deeply indigenous tradition can be discovered. The old beliefs did not go out overnight, as it were. Such was the basic unity of western European culture in the pre-Roman period, and so powerfully enshrined was it in the sub-conscious of the people, that elements continued uninterrupted, as indeed they probably do down to our own times. It is these aspects which seem to peer incongruously down from the roofs and walls of our churches, or take up their aggressive stance on the exterior of the buildings. The great long-necked gargoyles with foliage coming from their mouths, which characterize the exterior of so many cathedrals and churches, and the grotesque beasts and grinning masks, which can be detected high up on towers and spires, have a quality of movement and animation which is both impressive and sinister. We feel the old gods are still with us, in some thinly disguised form. Some of this feeling may stem from the age-old sanctity of *place*, the holy *locus*. There is a great corpus of evidence for the constant rededication of sanctuary-sites by successive incoming peoples or cults. Archaeology provides convincing evidence of this, and it becomes even more obvious when we enter the historical period. If you could throw down the old cult and canalize the powers of the local gods to your own ends this was obviously to your great benefit. Pope Gregory's famous instructions to St Augustine by Mellitus are noteworthy and apposite here:

> Do not pull down the fanes. Destroy the idols: purify the temples with *holy water*: set relics there, and let them become temples of the true God. So the people will have no need to change their places of concourse, and where of old they were wont to sacrifice cattle *to demons*, thither let them continue to resort on the day of the saint to whom the Church is dedicated, and slay their beasts, no longer as a sacrifice but for a social meal in honour of Him whom they now worship.

This gives the old faith an absolute reason for continuing, under a new nomenclature. And just as the pagan temple was set up in honour of a particular deity, so Christian churches were put under the aegis of special saints, with God as the ultimate force, lord of all. Like the Romans before them, the early Christians were good psychologists; they knew how to get the best out of both worlds by controlling, but canalizing, the powers of the old gods.

Over and above the sanctity of the *locus*, the holy place, and the power of its supernatural patron, there were numerous cult legends and deeply-rooted pagan symbols going back into an infinitely earlier European world which the Church would appear to have incorporated into its own dogma, with tact and tolerance, leaving the ultimate interpretation of the new forms to the worshippers. The subject of the human head is perhaps the widest and most important in its manifestations in the ecclesiastical and secular structures of Gothic Europe. Together with the cult of sacred springs and wells, the severed human head, or animal head, was one of the most worshipful of all the ancient pre-Christian symbols. Both were almost ineradicable. The cult of the head was taken into the Christian Church, and as a result the severed head is one of the most widespread and common motifs in the Gothic period. Grotesque heads are exceptionally numerous, as is the motif of the head with foliage coming from the mouth, or the human head mask embedded in greenery, the eyes staring balefully out, harking back to memories of human sacrifice and tree worship, widely practised in Europe, as elsewhere. The Celts, from whom so many of the later European peoples were descended, were, like other northern peoples, head-hunters. But apart from cutting off the heads of their enemies in battle they worshipped the severed head, and believed it to be imbued with every divine power—prophecy, fertility, speech, song and hospitality and, perhaps more than anything else, the power of averting evil. Thus, the presence of so many heads in our churches—janiform, tricephalic, foliate and purely grotesque—over and above the straightforward portrait heads, would have a very obvious explanation. In the same way heads set up on the gateposts of dwellings, or placed on walls or above doors, would have the same ultimate significance—the protection of the dwelling from evil forces, and the embuing of it with everything lucky and desirable. The classical writers commented in some detail on the Celtic cult of the human head, and how the Celts set heads up on gateposts or placed them in their temples, and covered them with gold and silver.

One has only to glance at the great corpus of La Tène art, the art of the pagan Celtic world between about 500 BC and the Roman period, to see the long ancestry of the foliate head. Many of the human masks on the superbly decorated metalwork of this highly subtle and sophisticated art are crowned with leaves or foliate motifs, or are seen against a background of the sacred tree itself. This is one motif which continues right through the Roman period in France and Britain to emerge again in medieval contexts, its ancestry fully apparent. Some of the heads and figures, and even altars, found in the Gothic churches are, in fact, actual pagan artefacts which were presumably found at the site of an earlier shrine or sanctuary, on which the Christian church was built, and incorporated into the latter structure as good luck symbols, probably after a purification rite had been carried out. In some instances they may have been taken to have been relics from an earlier Christian structure and given the name of a patron saint, or attributed to him.

In pagan contexts, again, the deity, male or female, often had a certain animal or bird as an attribute. Sometimes the deities took on the form of their cult creatures; sometimes they were portrayed as being composite with them; on occasion they were simply accompanied by them. Heads in which neither the bestial nor the anthropomorphic form seems to predominate may be derived from this ancient pagan concept of the composite deity.

Heads, then, are perhaps the most impressive feature of Gothic decoration, from the point of view of frequency of occurrence and the strange and numerous forms they take. Were we not in possession of a vast corpus of information and of artefacts which assure us of their long ancestry as evil-averting and decorative motifs in European contexts, we should be hard put to it to furnish ourselves with any satisfactory explanation for their presence in such numbers in our medieval churches and secular buildings.

Another common feature in the churches is the so-called tooth-ache figure. When the mouth is indicated or grasped by a single hand this interpretation might be the correct one, even though there is no proof. On the other hand, when two hands pull back the mouth into a fearful grimace, and the figure or bust is gigantic and sometimes double or triple, then it seems clear that we are dealing with that ancient and very long-lived and popular figure in European folklore, the giant. Giants have been believed in almost to the present day; the toponymy of Britain alone testifies to the role played by these supernatural beings. Until recently, while people still told stories round the fire, and every locality had its own legend and spectral familiars, the giant held a foremost place in the tradition. Not all giants were bad—some were kindly and beneficent towards mankind. Others were capricious, and a close eye had to be kept on them. A very interesting piece of what would seem to be actual evidence for the identification of these grim figures in our churches, pulling back fierce lips, or in the stern act of swallowing some hapless being, is the presence of several of these in the parish church at

Cerne Abbas, Dorset (*see* Giants). The hillside above this village is dominated by the ancient British giant *par excellence*, the Cerne Giant, cut deep in the turf to reveal the chalk below, representing a great divine figure, going back no one knows how far into the distant British past. The folklore of the locality has long commemorated his powers and his capacity to embue those who invoke him correctly with fecundity and prosperity. Echoes of this pagan god —huge in size as the gods and goddesses were always believed to be—are surely to be seen in the giants of Cerne Abbas church, just as are those of other local divinities, turned by folk belief into giants as a result of the disapproving influence of the Church, and placed inside or outside churches to be interpreted at will and in many different ways.

St George and St Michael were not the first dragon-slayers. The rider trampling down evil harks back in pagan iconography at least to Gallo-Roman times, and one cannot divine how much earlier it originated verbally as a cult legend in Europe. In northern and western Gaul in particular, isolated pillars, perhaps ultimately representing stylized trees, were erected. The pillar was surmounted by an elaborately carved capital, often decorated with foliage from which human masks or busts appear (*see* Foliate Heads), which formed the base for an equestrian statue of the triumphant Rider God, Taranis, 'The Thunderer', the Celtic equivalent of Jupiter. A giant with reptilian feet and legs is trampled beneath the horse's hooves, an agonized expression on its face. In one example at least the giant is double. Here on the so-called Jupiter Columns we have some now-irrecoverable myth about the conquest of the powers of darkness by the superior strength of the deities of the heavens. This cannot be so far from the St George myth, in which St George rides down and overcomes evil in the form of a fearful dragon.

Again, the widespread and deep-seated worship of a horned god is very well attested in the ancient pagan Celtic world, long before it emerged into an historical society. This cult figure, who may bear the horns of bull, ram or goat, or the stately antlers of the stag, is first found on rock-engravings in Scandinavia, northern Italy and southeastern France, dating to the second millennium BC or earlier. Later, he represents the benign aspects of a god of fertility and prosperity of every kind, commercial and agrarian. He seems to embody the tribal god in capacity as warrior, leader in war, conveyer of fecundity to people and to flocks and herds alike. He persists right through Roman contexts, where he would find sympathetic counterparts in the horned gods of the classical world. He re-emerges in medieval iconography, peering down from lofty roof-bosses and other situations, the foliage which sometimes emerges from his mouth or head linking him with his own silvan associations and with the Green Man and Foliate Head motifs. The very depth and power of his cult, and the longevity, would make him a natural symbol for the anti-Christ; that this was in fact the case is demonstrated by numerous popular representations of the Devil as a horn-bearing creature with hooves and tail.

Another common pagan motif was that of the severed head being devoured or gripped by the paw of some fearsome beast. Many examples of this motif in medieval church iconography can be closely paralleled in the imagery of Celtic and Romano-Celtic Europe. Sometimes a monster grasps two severed heads, one under each forepaw, sometimes it grasps a head between its paws. The sphinx is sometimes portrayed in this attitude. No matter what the context, pagan or Christian, the basic concept of this motif seems to lie in Man's constant awareness of dark spiritual forces which wait to snap him up and devour him, like some great ruthless monster. He employed every device he could to thwart these powers, and to gain the protection of his own gods, or God, as the case may be.

The Sheelagh-na-Gig, too, the enigmatic fertility figure, whose name cannot be satisfactorily translated and who is found in Ireland, Britain and on the Continent, requires explanation in ecclesiastical contexts, but this remains elusive. Sometimes the sexuality of the figure is crude and obvious to a degree, sometimes less marked; but the posture reveals the basic fertility imagery, characterized by the gesture indicating the genitalia, which are sometimes grossly exaggerated. Many of these figures are female, a few male. Various opinions of their original purpose have been proposed—that they were simply the whim of a coarse-minded craftsman, for example, or that they were reminders in a spiritual context of the sins of the flesh and its temptations. In Ireland, however, by no means all of these figures are found in religious buildings; and in Britain several have obviously been built into churches rather than forming a part of the essential structure, like a corbel or a boss.

Ancient Celtic mythology knew of a territorial goddess whose cult was widespread throughout Europe. In the early Irish tales we read that she was normally a radiantly lovely woman, dignified and desirable. But when she set out to prove the king-elect, who must mate with her before he could assume kingship, she turned herself into a hideous, sexual hag; all would refuse to sleep with her save he who was born to occupy the first place in the land. When the true king agrees to accept her repulsive advances, she changes back into her gracious form, and by her union with the ruler blesses his reign and protects the land from all evil and calamity. This seems a possible interpretation for these hideous fertility figures. The idea of the dual character of the earth goddess was widespread and fundamental in ancient Europe. If her powers were canalized for the good of the Christian faith she could be tolerated in churches and elsewhere in the medieval world. Her grossness would be calculated to keep the most fearsome forces at bay; her favour would ensure the good of the building and its prosperity.

Another extremely important pagan Celtic deity was Sucellos, 'The Good Striker', the mallet god. He, too, figures in Christian iconography under some new guise, as no doubt do many other members of the ancient Celtic pantheon.

However we are to interpret the great corpus of gargoyles and grotesques, and other seemingly pagan motifs, which enrich and enliven our European churches, one thing is clear. These strange devices cannot simply be written off as meaningless decorations of purely functional features. It is certain that many of them had a very real meaning for those who created them and for those who worshipped in the structures which housed them or were externally adorned by them. The repertoire is vast, the regional variation considerable. But underlying the whole complexity and range of subject and treatment is a basic quality which makes it possible for us to consider them as a group rather than as a series of independent, unrelated phenomena. The Church in medieval times had come to be the storehouse of the sub-conscious of the people—the lumber-room, as it were, in which were bygone, ancient, half-forgotten, half-formulated beliefs and superstitions, customs and folklore. The authorities would seem to have been remarkably tolerant of these, and by countenancing such bric-à-brac the Church has effectively preserved to an astonishing degree a great deal of our ancient past. Could we interpret it in all its complexity, a fascinating picture would no doubt become apparent. As it is, this small book attempts to indicate some fragment of the rich repertoire of imagery in the form of gargoyles and grotesques which the Church has collected for us, and to point out that, no matter what other cultural influences may have played a part in our Gothic iconography, the ancient beliefs of the peoples of pagan Europe must certainly be counted amongst these, and given due consideration.

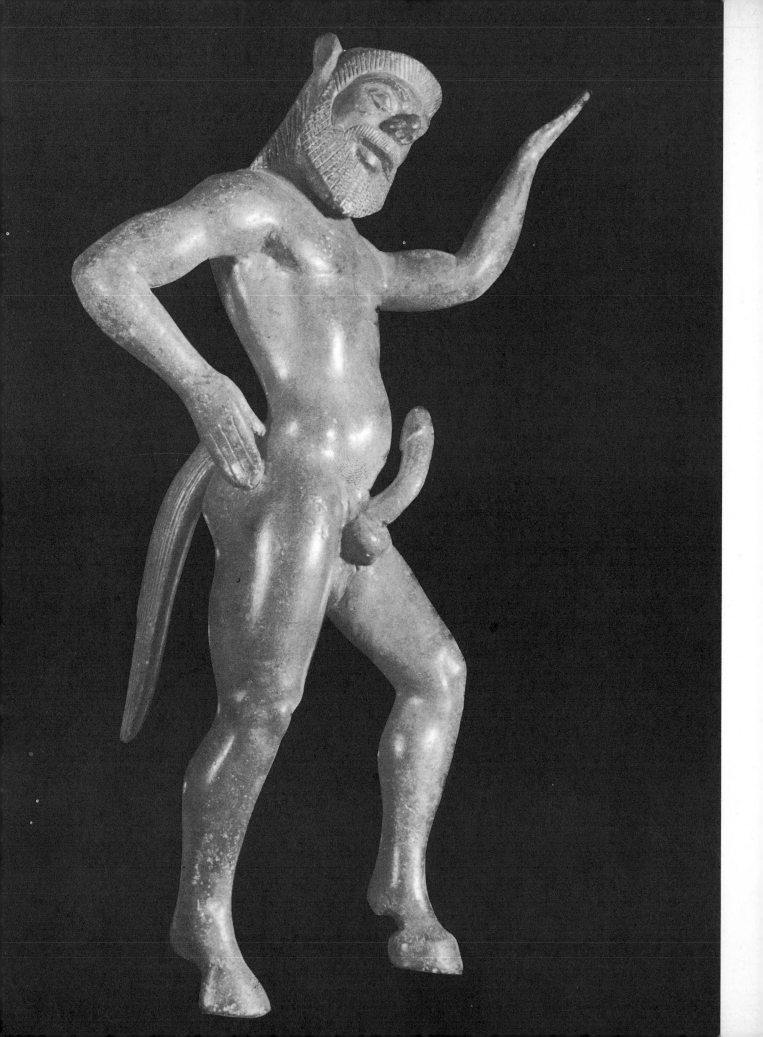

1 *Left*
Bronze figure of Pan, fifth century
BC, Athens National Museum
2 *Above*
Seventh century AD, harness
decoration in bronze from Sweden
3 *Right*
Voodoo mask of carved wood,
Nigeria

BEFORE LOOKING AT European grotesques, it is notable that at all periods of time and in all regions, Man has used the grotesque—horrific or benign—to symbolize his desire to avert the powers of evil and canalize the forces of good. This is clearly illustrated if we compare gargoyles from other, pagan, cultures with their Gothic counterparts. In these first examples, we range over several countries and eras, starting with a bronze portrayal of Pan (1), the classical god, patron of the animal world, benign and virile in spite of his goat's ears and tail and his repulsive, half-human features. Next, from a European Christian period (seventh century AD) but a pagan context, come biting, intertwined serpents (2), with beaked heads and complex decorations of spirals and circles; a Voodoo mask (3) with the withdrawn, death-like aspect reminiscent of some of the Celtic divine pagan heads, strong horns symbolizing fecundity and male power; a lion gargoyle from Greece (4)—gargoyles

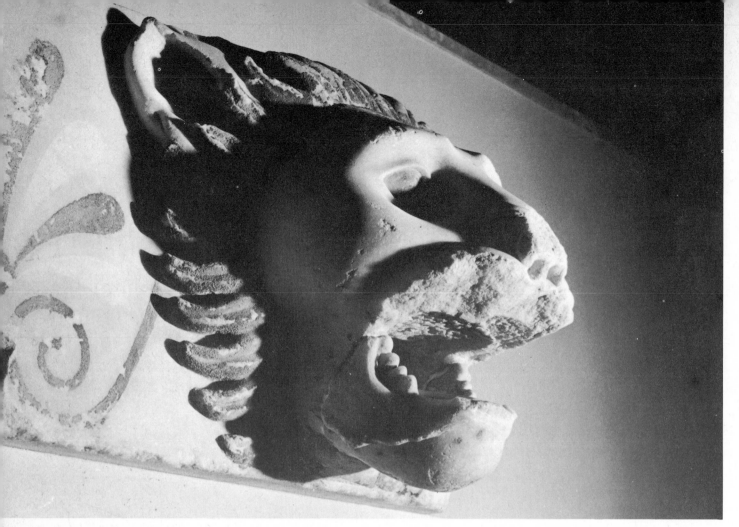

were no new invention of the medieval Church—which could find a place in many a later, ecclesiastical, context; a complex and terrifying portrait of Cocijo (5), the powerful Mexican raid-god, one of the blood-thirsty, death-dealing deities of that sacrifice-demanding religion, showing many features associated with the medieval Christian Church—the triple, foliage-like headdress, the huge head with deep holes for eyes, the grotesque, protruding tongue, the air of grim power, keeping at bay lesser spirits, demanding and obtaining sacrifice; and, finally, a Chinese emperor's coat (6), richly adorned with the great dragon, horned and grimacing, with gripping claws and lashing tail. All these use similar imagery to the gargoyles and grotesques which we have come to regard, perhaps wrongly, as an essential part of our Christian heritage, the meaning of which we can only dimly apprehend today.

4 *Above*
Marble gargoyle in the form of a lion, fifth century BC, Athens National Museum
5 *Below*
Cocijo, the Mexican rain god
6 *Right*
Chinese emperor's silk coat with dragon embroidered design

1 *Left*
The Cerne Abbas Giant on the hillside

Giants

The Cerne Giant has dominated the hillside above the village of Cerne Abbas for centuries (1). Some two hundred feet high, and cut deep through the turf into the chalk, he strides across the hillside, brandishing his club, proud in his virility. He has all the attributes of a good Celtic tribal god; physical strength, unblemished form, menacing, protective, his right arm raised to strike with his formidable weapon, his left arm stretched in an attitude of protective benediction. Who he really is we

25

shall probably never know—perhaps the tribal god of the Durotriges, the Celtic tribe who occupied this territory. There are certainly many parallels in Celtic tradition for a god of this kind; the Irish pagan god, the Dagda, for example, 'The Good God', with his great club and his capacity to supply his people with all their various needs. The Dagda was also called Ol-Athair, the all-father, guarding and shielding his children by his huge size and physical courage; with his crude virility he deals death with one blow of his mighty club, but also restores the victim to life with it. It was so huge that it had to be transported round Ireland on wheels, according to legend. In Gaul his equivalent was Sucellos, the Mallet God, 'The Good Striker'; the mallet replaces the club, and Sucellos holds the patera, or dish of plenty, whereby he nourishes his people. The Cerne Giant must have had some similar descriptive name attached to him in pagan times. In a medieval record he is called Helith, but we do not know how old or genuine this name is. He still plays a part in local folklore and custom, and until fairly recently at any rate was included in the premarital ritual of young people in the neighbourhood.

2, 3 *Left and above*
Cerne Abbas, Dorset—two of the four exterior carvings representing the Cerne Giant on the façade of the church

The Church must always have felt uneasy about this blatantly pagan figure, and yet his protective and menacing powers must have continued to receive credence, and the concept of such a deity must have been widely known. The Giant himself remains, with his frank virility, unchallenged, a landmark in the midst of the rich, undulating countryside which he still guards with his mighty club.

At Cerne Abbas church, not half a mile from the Cerne Giant itself, there is a series of carvings on the façade, which are recognizably the Giant. One is simply a figure holding a club, and is not necessarily a giant in itself, but it is accompanied by four smaller figures, making it a giant by comparison; the pagan gods are always represented as being much larger than human beings anyway.

In two of the carvings (3, 4) the smaller figures are holding the Giant's mouth open and in one final group (5) are seen to be helping the Giant to swallow a fourth figure. Surely this grim scene represents the giant's acolytes or priests engaged in sacrificing a human being to the god.

Stories of giants are widespread in British folklore; and there is a

whole repertoire of fearsome giant figures in our churches (3,6,7)—crude hands pulling back a huge mouth into a fearful, menacing gesture, sometimes as a single image and sometimes, as in the case of Cerne Abbas, flanked on either side by other, smaller figures, perhaps like the pagan Celtic idea of the power of the triadic form standing for the Giant in triple form, a most powerful and daunting concept. Sometimes the Giant uses his paw-like hands to push some hapless victim into his great maw. Portrayals of him are not confined to either the exterior or the interior of buildings—they may appear in either or both contexts. The great Giant of Cerne looks down on to Cerne Abbas church where his fierce counterparts adorn the façade, snarling menacingly out at the world and testifying to the deep-rooted nature of the tradition which did not destroy its pagan past, but blended it into Christian imagery so that all

4, 5 *Above and above right*
Cerne Abbas, Dorset—two of the exterior carvings on the façade of the church
6 *Below left*
Winchester—a roof boss 'giant' on the nave ceiling
7 *Below right*
Sherborne, Dorset—a misericord showing the Cerne Giant. In addition to the hands-to-mouth gesture, this carving is at least four times as large as any of the other figures carved on misericords in Sherborne Abbey

8 *Left*
Amesbury, Wiltshire—a carved
beam end showing the giant

possible supernatural forces were invoked and placated.

In York Minster there is a late Gothic representation of the giant, which shows the seated figure with his two small supporters behind his shoulders. The giant's stomach has become a glaring face with staring eyes and protruding tongue. Unlike earlier representations which have normal feet and hands, these figures have only dog-like claws, and the giant has been fitted with feathered wings. The intention is evidently to equate the pagan giant with Satan, and we can thus see how the transformation was made from pagan Celtic to Christian.

The Green Man, or Jack o' the Green

1 *Above*
Christchurch, Oxford—a roof boss

One of the most pagan and archiac concepts in the imagery of the Christian Church must be that of the so-called Green Man, or Jack o' the Green. Together with the Giant group it forms one of the most incontestably pre-Christian types. The Celts worshipped the human head; and in the La Tène period they often depicted a head or mask so intertwined with foliage that sometimes it is hard to see where the head ends and the branches and leaves begin. Sometimes these are stylized to form features of the face itself. The heads were also frequently given a crown of leaves. This is taken by experts in the subject to be a

symbol of divinity; thus, such heads would be those of powerful pagan deities, protecting and promoting growth and fertility, and the spirits of the trees the Celts so much venerated. The capital of a Jupiter column found at Cirencester, Gloucestershire (2,3,4,5), is decorated with two male and two female deities, all emerging from foliage.

In the Christian iconographic repertoire, this widespread motif grew in popularity in the fourteenth and fifteenth centuries (6–12). Foliage is often depicted growing from the mouth as well as from the crown of the head and the sides of the face. There are literally thousands of

2, 3, 4, 5 *Above*
Cirencester, Gloucestershire—the four faces of the Jupiter column, third century AD
6, 7 *Above right and right*
Canterbury, Kent—roof bosses in the cloisters

32

8 *Left*
Dorchester, Oxfordshire—a corbel
overlooking the altar
9 *Above right*
Assisi, Italy—an exterior capital
10 *Right*
Doge's Palace, Venice—detail
from a capital in an upper gallery

roof-bosses containing this theme, which is thought to derive from May Day rites, with their pagan origin and fertility connection. May Day was one of the great calendar festivals of the pagan Celtic year, and the genuine celebrations survived in England even to the end of the nineteenth century. In the Middle Ages the cult must have been even more meaningful and widely practised, and the Church was always fighting a losing battle against tree-worship, which would seem to have been as deeply rooted in the traditions of the people as well-worship, equally abhorred by the Church. The prac-

tice of dancing round the sacred tree continued for centuries; sometimes it was extended to dancing round the church, to the considerable concern of the clergy. In medieval England the chief player, male or female, in these fertility rites was masked with foliage.

11 *Above left*
Canterbury, Kent—roof bosses in the cloisters
12 *Right*
Dover, Kent—spire decorations

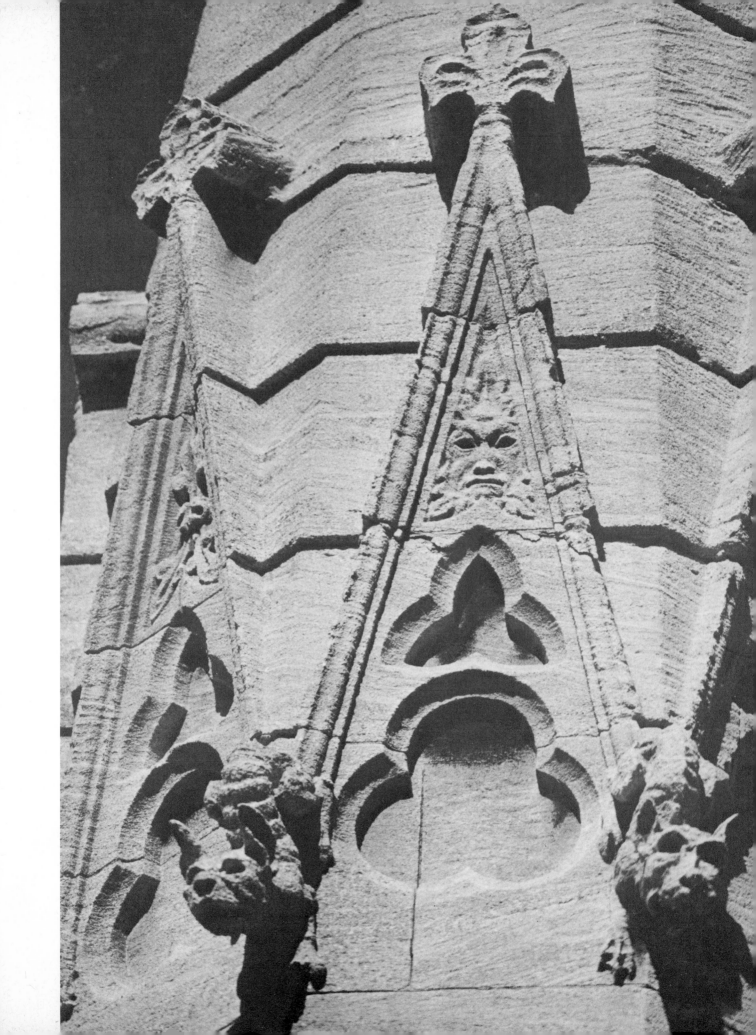

Foliate Heads

Closely linked to the Green Man theme is that of the innumerable foliate heads, animal, human or a combination of both, which form one of the most popular motifs in the medieval church. In many cases the oak is depicted, significantly, because this was the tree sacred to the Druids and most revered of all trees by the pagan Celts. In this group the foliage sometimes grows directly from the mouth while the head itself does not sprout greenery, as in an example from Oberstenfeld, Germany (1). On some examples the head is that of an animal, such as a cat, as in an example from Studenica, Yugoslavia (3). Here bifurcated branches spring from the mouth to merge into the surrounding decoration, and foliate motifs from the crown of the head curve down the sides. The eyes, with

deeply-drilled pupils, are fixed and menacing. A wooden beast-head which is so closely intertwined with its foliate decoration that it is difficult to separate the two is in Westminster Abbey (2). The nostrils and fangs of the beast are formed from coiled greenery, the eyes by spirals of foliage. Horns and antlers are suggested by the leaves which spring from the crown and between the eyes; and the whole forms a good example of the total integration of the two entities—beast and sacred tree. Here we are indeed in the presence of ancient pagan belief in the power and spirit of the tree. This is also the case with an impressive example from Vienna (4). The sombre, semi-human head with its flat crown and flowing moustaches has two branches of foliage springing

1 *Left*
Oberstenfeld, Germany—detail from a capital in the nave
2 *Below*
Westminster Abbey—misericord in the Henry VII Chapel

from the mouth, each converging to
form a subtle decorative theme on
either side of the head. The nose is
flat and somewhat muzzle-like; the
brows, which add to the scowling expression, merge boldly upwards into
the fur-like hair above. The great
paw-like hands grow directly from
the head and grasp the ends of the
stonework below. Another head from
Vienna (5) is in less bestial form. The
deeply-drilled eyes and the hatched
brows again convey an intense staring gaze, sharply contrasting with
the gloomy but more naturalistic

3 *Above*
Studenica, Yugoslavia—an
exterior panel detail
4, 5 *Above right and right*
St Stephen's, Vienna, Austria—
exterior decorations in a doorway

6 *Above*
Kilpeck, Herefordshire—an
exterior capital
7 *Left*
Troyes, France—an exterior detail
in a doorway
8 *Right*
Sens, France—a capital in a nave

faces below on either side, which are themselves covered by the branches springing from either side of the 'deity's' mouth. The whole is completely integrated with the foliage, and once again the concept of the powerful spirit of the sacred tree or grove is evidenced.

Another impressive and essentially non-naturalistic head is at Kilpeck, Herefordshire (6), where there is an extremely rich repertoire of grotesques of every kind (*see* Kilpeck). This example, with its clear Celtic derivation, has heavy, decorative brows, and deeply-drilled pupils in the double-outlined eyes. From the great gaping, fish-like mouth spring two branches bearing fruit and decorated in a manner similar to the brows. Below is a twisted circle of stones, reminiscent of a Celtic torc or neck-ring. Another semi-human bestial head is at Troyes, Aube, France (7). It has flaring, Silenus-like nostrils, scowling brows, bull-horns, and a tuft of hair in the centre of the forehead. From either side of the figure-of-eight-shaped mouth spring branches with leaves and fruit. The horned god— bull, ram or goat—was one of the oldest and most widely spread of the pagan Celtic deities. He often portrayed fecundity, and his connection with woodlands is attested by his equation, on occasion, with Silvanus, Roman god of the woods. Another fierce, half-human, half-leonine head merges with lush oak foliage at Sens, Yonne, France (8). The fierce eyes have deeply-drilled pupils; the moustache is stylized, the nose thick and bulbous with emphatic nostrils. The brow is furrowed, adding to the impression of fierceness. The even teeth seem to bite on the two branches of oak which grow from the drawn-back mouth to form the surrounding decoration.

Cernunnos

One of the most ancient and widespread deities worshipped all over pagan Celtic Europe was the horned god; he is often associated with a serpent. In Christian contexts he was frequently made to represent the devil, or other forces of evil. As in earlier, pagan contexts he is portrayed as a head with surprising frequency in Christian iconography. Sometimes he is only horned, and sometimes he has serpents sprouting from his mouth or head. On occasion he is seen with both. Whatever the significance of these heads in the imagery of the Church, it is clear what their symbolism would be to the congregation of the Middle Ages and later periods. The crude, sinister power would be symbolic of all the forces which battled constantly against Christianity for the possession of the soul. They would both serve as a fearful warning and, by their very powerful grimaces, be thought able to keep hostile evil powers at bay. The pagan Celts used to set up severed human heads in their sanctuaries and houses for this purpose.

A magnificent ram-horned head with a grimacing, gap-toothed mouth, comes from Schwäbisch Gmünd, Germany (1). The beard sprouts into long, comma-shaped strands on either side of the mouth, leaving the square chin bare. The nose is flat, with broad fleshy lobes. Lines on the brow, which seems to

give the impression of being covered by a tuft of sheep's wool, convey a fierce scowling impression which must have been very intimidating to the superstitious mind. From the same church comes another complex horned head (2), bull-horned this time, with a similar flat nose with boldly-depicted lobes, and lentoid eyes carved in a very archaic fashion. From the huge open mouth, filled with jagged teeth, emerge two coiled snakes with heads of calves or some similar animals pointing upwards with intense expression. From Assisi, Umbria, Italy, comes a wood carving of a demoniac horned head showing very complex imagery (3). This has become merged with the foliate mask concept, and we see broad leaves

1, 2 *Above left and above* Schwäbisch Gmünd, Germany— two carvings placed inside the church at the rear end, both figures looking up the length of the building towards the altar

emerging from either side of the ram-horned head. The huge mouth is pulled back and opened, to produce a hideous snarl and reveal the tongue, teeth and fangs. The nose is broad and flat. The scowling brow is decorated by a leaf from either side of which several deep lines are drawn. The drooping moustaches curl round stiffly at the ends; the pupils of the malevolent eyes are depicted by a spiral motif. Double lines lead from the outer sides of the eyes to tufts of fur at either side of the head, while foliate ears rest on the curves of the horns. Behind the horns other features appear to indicate a second pair.

A less dramatically horrific, but nevertheless highly sinister head is carved in the church at Lowick, Northumberland (4). The top part of the head is square in shape, and would appear to have stylized, curving ram-horns as well as vestigial horns on the top of the crown separated by a tuft of wool. The beard, moustaches and side whiskers are depicted in flowing, naturalistic style, like those of some classical river-god. The nose has bulging, Silenus-like lobes; the lentoid eyes are blank and non-committal. The naturalistically-depicted mouth and rounded chin somehow manage to convey a much more subtle impression than do the more overtly fearsome masks described above. Two bull-horned figures from Dreieichen, Austria (7), are also in this tradition. The horns are laid flat across the brow, with no clear separation by hair; the figures grasp their horns with fleshy hands attached to arms

growing directly from the sides of the heads. With thick, down-turned mouths, accentuated by beards and moustaches depicted by straight lines, and with wide, lentoid eyes with deeply-drilled pupils, their expression emphasized by the hollowed-out brow-line which runs unbroken across the top of the somewhat thick and coarse nose, they glare down in a manner calculated to alarm anyone happening to catch their baleful stare. Much more complex is a horned head from Bitonto, Apulia, Italy (5). The crown of the head recalls a scallop-shell. From below this spring two ram-horns decorated with lines like twisted seashells; from either side of the broad, coarse nose with wide nostrils grows an upturned formal moustache which, in fact, is made up of foliage, linking this head with the Jack of the Green series. The ears are animal; the mouth, shaped like a figure of eight, holds what appears to be part of a ring (*see* Hagodays).

A head in the direct pagan Celtic tradition, at Kilpeck, Herefordshire (*see* Kilpeck), has lentoid eyes with deep holes for pupils and a flat nose with bored nostrils (6). The huge mouth is wide open, the tongue composed of two serpents which rise to frame the face. The serpents' tongues connect the two beak-like mouths on the top of the head.

5 *Left*
Bitonto, southern Italy—stone
carved decoration over a door
6 *Above*
Kilpeck, Herefordshire—detail
from the archway
7 *Right*
Dreieichen, Austria—exterior
column capital. The figures
resemble Nobodies (see page 112)

49

Creatures Devouring Heads

This motif, which appears frequently in cathedrals and churches, goes right back in pre-Christian Celtic iconography to the theme of beasts devouring a human head which is found all over early Europe. In an example from Noves, France, probably dating to the first century BC, a fearful beast holds an expressionless, bearded male head under each paw while gripping a human figure in its jaws (1). The head and legs are both now broken off and lost, though the fractured surfaces remain at either side of the jaws, but proof that it was a human figure is to be seen in the arm wearing a bracelet which still exists and hangs from below the jaws, extending to meet the beast's right paw. There is also a broken stump attached to the left paw.

This pagan sculpture, so powerfully and brilliantly executed, a major work of art by any standard, at the same time attests the strength and sophistication of pagan religious practice in the period immediately before the arrival of the Christian Church.

The Colchester sphinx, one of the finest Romano-British sculptures, comprises a powerful sphinx gripping the large severed head of a man. Both the above are themes much used in the medieval religious iconography, in direct follow-through from the pagan forms. From Sens, Yonne, France, comes an impressive representation of a head, naturalistic in form, with the sombre, remote expression of many of the pagan Celtic severed heads (2). The griffin-like creatures which flank it and appear to be about to devour it grasp the foliate motif at the base with powerful, triple-clawed feet. A left hand apparently belonging to the head grips a beast's claw; the foliage forms a decorative element, merging with the scene. From Millstatt, Austria (*see also* Column Figures), a similar scene occurs on the capital of a column (3). Two formidable lions, their tails in traditional positions, seize the open mouth of a bearded head with their paws. They are devouring the head with apparent avidity, the whole upper part being inside their mouths. Their eyes, noses and fur are treated in the same manner as the hair, eyes and nose of the head. Once again, foliage blends with this ancient motif.

1 *Left*
The 'Tarascon de Noves'—a first-century BC sculpture of the Celtic 'La Tene' period
2 *Above right*
Sens, France—capital in the nave
3 *Right*
Millstatt, Austria—a column in the cloisters

Non-naturalistic Severed Heads

The pre-Christian Celts worshipped the human head; like other northern peoples, they were head-hunters. But over and above cutting off the heads of defeated enemies and preserving them for display purposes, the Celts worshipped the human head and made images of it in a great variety of media. Sometimes these divine heads were represented in a more or less naturalistic manner, although the expressions are invariably remote and non-portrait-like. Sometimes the heads are double, or janiform, and sometimes triple, or tricephalic. The number three was sacred to the Celts; to portray a god-head with three faces or three heads was to give the image an invincible power and perfection. These tricephaloi are portrayed in pre-Christian iconography in a variety of ways. The motif was

taken into the Christian Church to portray the Trinity; but this device was frowned upon by the Church authorities, and eventually banned. Hundreds of extremely interesting examples of the severed head motif are to be seen in churches and cathedrals all over Europe; the device of setting up a severed head or an image of one was adopted widely in Christian times. Indeed, the motif of the head in its various forms, originating in the pre-Christian era, might be described as the most prolific of all the motifs found in Christian iconography.

A fine example of a janiform head decorates a roof-boss in Canterbury Cathedral, Kent (1). The two heads are placed side by side rather than back to back. Three eyes serve for the two faces; in pre-Christian Celtic

contexts two eyes may serve for three faces, the central face being flanked on either side by profile faces. There are also only three eyebrows here, but two noses, mouths and beards. The brow is smooth and sweeping. A tricephalos at York Minster (2) has three faces each with its own full complement of features. The central face, flanked by identical faces in semi-profile, gazes out over the building with a profound, all-knowing look. The heads are crowned by a scroll-like feature which may stand for diadems or stylized horns. From Landshut, Germany, so close to the cradle of the Celtic Iron Age, come strings of pointed male heads (3), the beards of rope-like texture forming part of the design and linked one with another. The heads are all very similar to each other, the rope-like quality of the beards being echoed in the similar portrayal of the moustaches. The eyes are lentoid in shape, the mouths straight, and the hair depicted by a series of wavy lines.

1 *Left*
Canterbury—roof boss in the cloisters
2 *Above*
York Minster, the Chapter House
3 *Right*
Landshut, Germany—linked heads in an archway

Heads with Protruding Tongues

An extraordinary number of grotesque heads are depicted with protruding tongues. The exact significance of this gesture can only be surmised. It may be intended merely to increase the crude and menacing appearance of these heads, which often also have foliage protruding from their mouths. On the other hand the significance of the motif may be more subtle. The exposure of the genitalia was widely believed to thwart and keep at bay pursuing evil forces (*see* Fertility). The protruding tongue may have been believed to have similar powers, and thus these grim and fearsome heads peering down from some lofty corner of a sacred building may have been intended not to intimidate worshippers but to keep the ever-pressing demoniac forces firmly under control. A very fine series of such heads appears on roof-bosses in the cathedral at Canterbury, Kent (2, 5). Semi-bestial, semi-human, the bright paintwork emphasizing their fearsome features, their tongues fully protrude from their fangs, while their eyes glare down under scowling brows which sometimes bear foliate hair. Another (4) forms part of the external decoration of the church at Barfreston, Kent. Deeply-drilled pupils add to the intense staring quality of the eyes, while the tongue protrudes from the huge, drawn-back mouth. A strange example of an animal with protruding tongue can be seen at Elham, Kent (1). An elongated, dog-like creature prowls along the wooden-frieze, its looped, barbed tail exactly matching the barbed tongue hanging from the great

1 *Below*
Elham, Kent—detail from a carved wooden fireplace beam; the building was originally an abbey
2 *Right*
Canterbury—roof boss in the cloisters

toothed mouth. Another interesting example occurs at Ault Hucknall, Derbyshire (3). The tongue protrudes but the lower part of the face is not represented. Above the pupil-less eyes, with their almond-shaped sockets, and the finely modelled nose are motifs which can be traced back to Celtic motifs dating to the La Tène period in Europe.

3 *Left*
Ault Hucknall, Derbyshire—gilded wooden beam end
4 *Top*
Barfreston, Kent—exterior carving under the eaves
5 *Above*
Canterbury—roof boss in the west porch

Glaring Creatures

1 *Above*
Brussels—gargoyle in the Grand Place

This group of creatures has clear affinities with the previous one; these menacing, leering creatures laugh without humour, or draw back their lips in an attitude of intimidation and grotesque terror. From Brussels comes a remarkable leonine creature with semi-human appearance (1), the closely clasped arms taut between powerful hind legs, the gaping, toothed mouth and the bulging, open eyes terrible in appearance. An example at Barfreston, Kent (3), is particularly interesting. The nostrils are formed from spiral designs which flow upwards from the figure-of-eight mouth: the eyes have deeply-drilled pupils which add to the impressive intensity of their stare. The ears are apparently feline, and the stylized fur between them is so arranged as to form a pattern. From the same church comes another glaring head (*see* back cover) which ends with the immense mouth, the lower part of the face being completely absent. This head appears to wear a slightly peaked cap, and there is a suggestion that once again the ears are animal. The almond-shaped eyes are defined by double lines, the brows low and menacing. The total aspect is grim and repellent. Clearly this was a most horrific image, intended to intimidate the most potent forces of darkness that might

beset the building and those who frequented it. Utterly horrific in their form are three heads in Canterbury Cathedral, Kent (2). Two smaller heads flank a larger, and we seem to have a variant on the tricephalic concept. The flanking heads have skull-like proportions, their faces ending with the lower jaw, the mouth drawn back in a fearsome snarl and filled with huge teeth. The noses are lacking, the deeply-drilled nostrils enhancing the skull-like impression. The eyes, which are not drilled, are prominent and round, glaring outwards with a clear ferocity. The central head, now badly worn, would seem to be of the same type. The

2 *Above*
Canterbury—exterior carving on the south wall
3 *Right*
Barfreston, Kent—exterior carving in a doorway

great gaping mouth and the prominent eyes can still be distinguished. From either side of the crown spring features which seem to be a blend of foliage and antlers. If we can allow antlers here, then we must be in the presence of the ancient Celtic god Cernunnos, whose cult goes back to the fifth century BC, if not earlier, and who was made a model for the anti-Christ, with his antlers and his ram-horned serpent attribute. Cernunnos was known all over continental Europe and the British Isles; his presence at Canterbury as a cautionary tale, as it were, would not be in any way unexpected. This is one of the most deeply pagan groups we witness in this volume.

From Sweden comes this glaring, very bristly boar (5). Painted on a wall in the church of Häuke Berga, it seems to stand for some mythological pig of the ancient world, alert, fierce, awaiting combat with impatience and eagerness. Another example of this motif of glaring heads or creatures is at Winchester, Hampshire (4). Here, tucked away in a convenient corner of the cathedral is a ravaging, fearsome leonine beast, paws tense, fanged mouth open and menacing, double-rimmed eyes gazing not downwards, but upwards. into eternity.

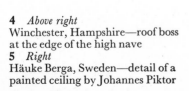

4 *Above right*
Winchester, Hampshire—roof boss at the edge of the high nave
5 *Right*
Häuke Berga, Sweden—detail of a painted ceiling by Johannes Piktor

Biting Creatures

This group consists of what we may consider to be the personification of a plague which besets our churches as much today as it did in medieval times—the Death-Watch Beetle. The biting creatures are consuming the very fabric of the church. There may also be an allegory here. That they all do their work with apparent relish is evident from their expression of grim pleasure as they mouth a beam or a column. Creatures biting living things are also to be included in this category. To begin with mon-sters devouring the structure, at Canterbury Cathedral, Kent (1), we have a gleeful head, its grinning mouth filled with fanged teeth, bliss-fully chewing away at a column, its raised eyes and sensuous nose with deeply-drilled nostrils all testifying to its complete oblivion to anything other than its pleasure in de-struction—perhaps a motif used in order to keep at bay the true destroyers of the fabric. Canterbury has a splendid repertoire of this motif, as of others. A less cheerful

1 *Left*
Canterbury—a roof boss in the cloisters
2 *Above*
Barfreston, Kent—rose window; on each 'spoke' of the wheel there is a carved head

61

biting head, with teeth but no fangs (3), chews away a wooden column with dedicated determination. The painted eyes again do much to emphasize the destructive nature of these creatures. Another, and very sinister, half-human head at the same cathedral viciously grasps the wood between its fangs and teeth and is obviously intent upon destruction. The hair forms strands which rise upwards, almost like sun-rays. The nose is coarse, with deeply depicted nostrils, and the eyes have a malevolent sort of glee about them which makes this one of the most impressively sinister examples in this category.

Another version of this motif, in stone, at Autun Cathedral, Saône et Loire, France (5), attacks the column which it surmounts. The small, hooded eyes focus on the column grasped by snarling lips. The nose is depicted in a series of wavy lines, the hair rises up to form solar-type rays. A horn springs from either side of the head, linking this object with one of the oldest pagan cults in Europe. At Barfreston, Kent, there is a whole galaxy of biting heads, eight of them munching the cylindrical shafts or spokes of the superb wheel-shaped window in the western gable (2). Some of these are badly weathered, others in a better state of preservation. One or two of the heads eat their column with a glum expression, while others appear to use their toothy mouths with a vigorous malevolence. Also at Barfreston is a creature biting not the fabric of the structure but another creature (4). The grim, owl-like head holds a rabbit or hare in its rapacious beak, its human eyes with deeply-drilled pupils staring pitilessly out from the wall of this enchanting and strange church.

3 *Left*
Canterbury—a roof boss in the cloisters
4 *Right*
Barfreston, Kent—an exterior carving under the eaves, with human-like ears and eyes
5 *Below*
Autun, France—column capital in the entrance

1 *Left*
Kilpeck, Herefordshire—carving on an exterior wall under the eaves
2 *Right*
Millstatt, Austria—this group is in the cloisters which connect the church with the old convent building and is only four feet from ground level. The nose has suffered some damage, but the tongue has not

Fertility

Amongst all the varied imagery of the medieval Church the frankly sexual or erotic figures are some of the most curious. The exposure of the genitalia was supposed to be an evil-averting act, and it may be that this was the significance of these figures. Again, they may have formed part of the teaching of the Church against sensuality, but in this case such crude figuration would surely have been potentially dangerous in arousing, rather than repressing, such carnal feelings. But whatever their ultimate significance, there is in fact a large repertoire of obscene carvings in Christian iconography, among which must be counted the Sheelagh-na-Gig. This type of figure, common in Ireland and found in churches in Britain and on the Continent, is hag-like and coarse, and indicates her genitals with her hands. A fine example can be seen at St Michael's Church, Oxford (6), another at Kilpeck, Herefordshire (1). The latter, like so much of the imagery at this church (*see* Kilpeck), is very archaic in appearance, and probably stems directly from Irish tradition. The round eyes with deeply-drilled pupils, the crudely indicated nose and the lack of mouth are very typical, as are the grotesquely enlarged genitalia, of the type of fertility figure found in so many Irish churches, or carved on slabs out on the moors, at cross-roads for example. These female figures may well represent the Celtic fertility or

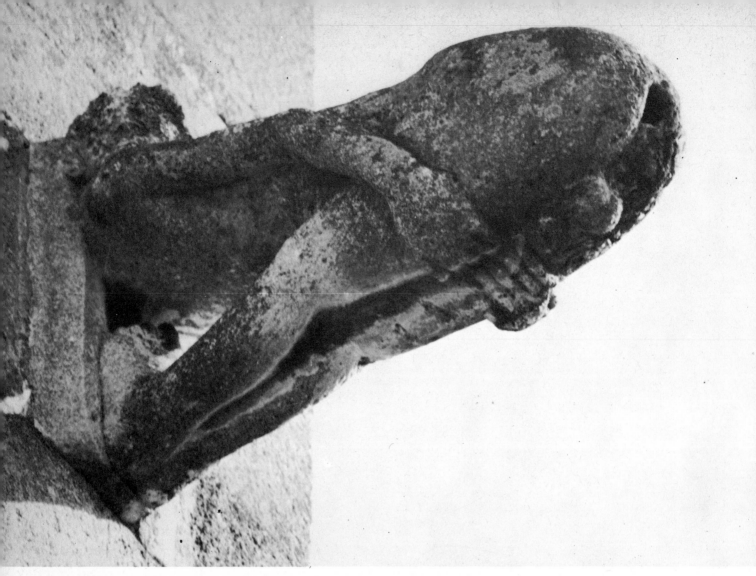

territorial goddess who, as the early tales tell us, was ritually mated with the king-elect in the guise of a hideous and sexual old hag who became a most lovely woman when the king consented to have intercourse with her. The feet are here rudimentary and paw-like, the hands large and coarse.

Another crudely erotic figure adorns the outside of the cathedral at Autun, Saône et Loire, France (3). A naked male bends down so that his head is on the ground. With his hands he parts the tops of the legs to reveal the testicles and gaping anus. No doubt his posture is one intended to drive away the ever-present forces of darkness by the power of the exposed sexual organs. A complex scene (2) at Millstatt church,

Austria (*see* Column Figures), comprises two figures, one a large animal of peculiar appearance, possibly a lion, the other a human wearing a skirt and so possibly female. The human figure, straddling the beast facing the rear, inserts the tongue between the buttocks which it forces apart with the hands. Another figure, suggestive of this range of fertility figures, is at Dreieichen, Austria (4), the arms raised in the manner of a caryatid, the legs splayed and bent upwards at the back. Yet another (5) is at Autun Cathedral, seated in a roundel, legs apart, the deeply-drilled pupils giving an air of wide-eyed innocence to this strange little creature.

66

3 *Above left*
Autun, France—gargoyle on the back wall of the church. Most of the other gargoyles on this building have been 'restored' and are quite unlike this remaining original one

4 *Above*
Dreieichen, Austria—carving on an exterior wall under the eaves

5 *Above right*
Autun, France—roundel from doorway decoration

6 *Right*
St Michael's, Oxford—a carved stone block, badly weathered. It must have been outside originally but is now kept in a box inside the church

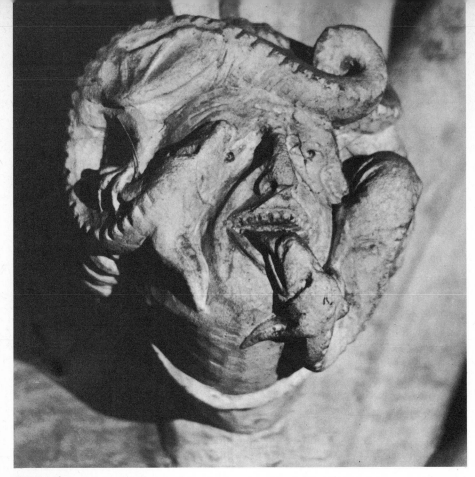

Nightmares

Another group of grotesques would seem best to deserve this classification; the subject matter is certainly the stuff of which nightmares are made. The imagery, both complex and horrific, is well represented at York Minster. One example, forming an impressive roof-boss (2), depicts a circular male face, the countenance mask-like in spite of the attentions of two grim, dove-like birds which clasp the head in their claws and are avidly engaged in pecking the nostrils. Foliage springs from the crown of the head to form a cap of leaves. The face bears a certain similarity to the splendid male face from the Romano-Celtic temple at Bath, Somerset, dedicated to the Celtic goddess Sulis. Here the copious locks are composed of weed-like and serpentiform elements, appropriate to a water deity; the lentoid eyes with sharply-defined pupils stare out from the remains of the portico which this sculpture must have adorned with much grandeur. At York too, an agonized demoniac face, lips drawn back in a ghastly snarl, eyes narrowed, hair in stiff strands, suffers beneath a monstrous creature perching on its brow, gripping with terrible claws, peering out into the church with baleful eyes, the huge mouth leering open to display vicious, jagged teeth (3). An equally nightmarish composition adorns another roof-boss (1). Three reptiles with lamb-like heads devour the tongue and eyes of a human head which they grip with relentless claws. They coil about the top of the head giving the viewer an impression of horns. It must be recalled that in North Britain a horned god was widely worshipped in pre-Christian times; and that the ram-headed serpent was one of his most frequent attributes, here and in continental Europe. There must have been a great deal of blending of

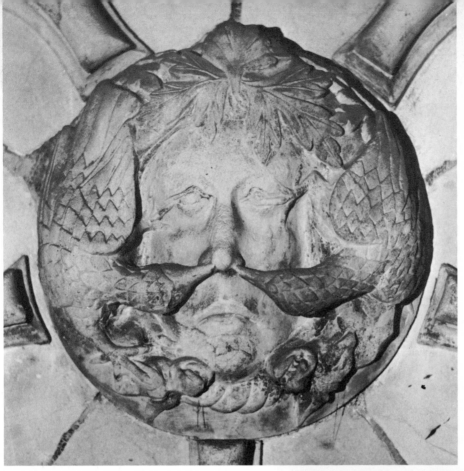

indigenous traditions with motifs derived from a variety of alien sources, combining to give an impression and convey a message which is now beyond all but our vaguest comprehension. Another nightmare creature, with a lamb-like head comparable to those on the York boss, forms a roof-boss at Canterbury Cathedral, Kent. Here the limbs are awkwardly arranged in an unnatural position, the creature staring downwards in a blank yet sinister way.

Beaked Heads and Associated Pantheon

Some of the most interesting features of medieval architecture are the richly-decorated doorways, with their infinite variety of recurring motifs. The regularity with which some motifs occur is suggestive of some set of traditions, indeed of a whole pantheon, whose significance is now lost to us. One recurrent theme is the row of beak-heads, often half horse-like in appearance, half bird-like. That this motif of a winged, beaked horse goes back to the pagan Celtic period is well attested by, for example, a very lively bronze roundel from Santon Downham, Suffolk (3), which portrays just such a creature. Fine examples, from Romanesque contexts, of this semi-equine, semi-avian creature are at St Ebbe's, Oxford (2), and at Asthall, Oxfordshire (1,11); there is a splendid example at Kilpeck, Herefordshire (10), rich in imagery (*see* Kilpeck) where much of the iconography would seem to hark back to earlier, native, traditions.

There is an infinite satisfaction in

1 *Left*
Asthall, Oxfordshire—a beak head from the doorway. This head, unlike plate 11, is rather more bird-like than horse-like
2 *Above*
St Ebbe's, Oxford—a complete arch of beak heads now dismantled from the building. Note that the head third from right and the head third from left are identical in design to the two beak heads illustrated from Asthall
3 *Below*
Santon Downham, Suffolk—Roman period bronze roundel, first century AD

71

the variations on the basic theme of beak-headed creatures, and the figures which accompany them, on some of the great elaborate doorways; at Tickencote, Rutland (9), for example, or Healaugh, Yorkshire (6), or Adel, Yorkshire (4, 5, 8). Amongst the menacing severed heads on the Adel arch many are devouring other creatures. Two of the latter

4, 5 *Above left and above right*
Adel, Yorkshire—details of an arch dividing the nave from the apse
6 *Below*
Healaugh, Yorkshire—double decorated arch, beak heads inside, the outer carrying a whole pagan pantheon. Note foliate head second from left

7 *Below*
Kilpeck, Herefordshire—
carved head from the archway of
the west door. This is one of a
repeated series of similar heads
around this arch, all of which are
upside-down

have mask-like faces characteristic of
earlier Celtic sculptures, and are
being snapped up by the teeth of a
huge-eyed head. Here, too, are most
interesting examples of the Celtic
tricephalic motif, the triple heads;
among the examples shown is a
horned animal head surmounted by
two bearded human heads. The variety and nature of the details of these

arches of beak-heads and the figures which go with them is extremely intriguing and provocative. The motifs of snapping, biting heads, semi-human and semi-animal; the entwining serpents sometimes forming the tongue or double tongue of the head (Kilpeck, 7); the motifs of birds and the strange, beaked creatures—all recur in such a way as to suggest that a whole lost mythology is enshrined in them, complex and remote and perpetually fascinating.

8 *Above*
Adel, Yorkshire—detail of the arch dividing the nave from the apse
9 *Below*
Tickencote, Rutland—the great multi-arched span inside the church dividing nave from apse, the inner arch being all beak heads whilst the middle arch comprises no less than forty different representations, not one of which is identifiably Christian

10 *Right*
Kilpeck, Herefordshire—beak head detail. Note that this beak head is one of only a few such on the Kilpeck arch (*see* Kilpeck, plate 1)

11 *Below*
Asthall, Oxfordshire—a beak head from the doorway. This head has a harness suggesting horse rather than bird

1 *Left*
Barfreston, Kent—a capital
2 *Below*
Vienna—decoration in the south doorway
3 *Right*
St Mark's, Venice—carving at a corner of the main façade

Bi-corporates and Animalistic Polycephali

Another interesting series of grotesques comprises the motifs of the single head from which two bodies grow and that of multiple animal heads. In a fine example of the bicorporate motif which comes from Vienna (2) a grim-faced human head surmounts two griffin-like bodies which grip the architecture with their firm claws and twine their tails about the foliage which forms part of the decoration. The bicorporate motif would seem to be a variant on the motif of the two beasts devouring a severed human head; sometimes the bicorporate is indeed engaged in this activity. A splendid example from St Mark's, Venice (3), shows a fearsome, human-headed bicorporate lion, with staring eyes and wide open mouth, gripping between its paws the head of an animal—just as in the Roman period more naturalistic lions are portrayed devouring the head of a ram. Another bicorporate consists of a fierce lion-like creature with open mouth and protruding tongue. Yet another of this genre comes from Barfreston church, Kent (1). Here the open mouth gives forth foliage instead of a tongue, which swells to

form the base upon which the double creature crouches. A very peculiar bicorporate in the shape of a lamb-like animal forms one of the splendid roof bosses in Canterbury Cathedral, Kent (7). A most sinister example (4) comes from Millstatt, Austria (*see* Column Figures). Here the crouched, double-bodied leonine beast is in the act of swallowing a human head, a pair of hands, which presumably belong to this, hanging helplessly on either side of the monster's chin. The mouth of the head being swallowed is naturalistic and tranquil, in contrast to the fierce mask-like head of the beast dominating and destroying it.

Canterbury Cathedral contains some fine examples of the bestial polycephalic motif. One (6) comprises three leonine heads with chins

4 *Above far left*
Millstatt, Austria—cornice
decoration
5 *Left*
Canterbury—a roof boss in the
nave
6, 7 *Below left and right*
Canterbury—roof bosses in the
cloisters

meeting and tongues uniting to form
a foliate design. Another shows a
similar motif, with fierce lamb-like
heads, tongues conjoined in the same
fashion. A splendid boss from the
same building (5) has a semi-human,
semi-leonine double head with
shared, gaping mouth and flamboy-
ant nostrils.

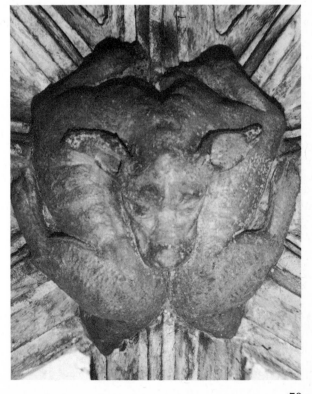

Hermaphrodites

Bi-sexual or hermaphrodite figures also occur in the rich repertoire of gargoyles and grotesques. Several of these carved in wood are in Canterbury, Kent. One depicts a male head, probably horned (1), with bristling moustaches. The upper part of the face is janiform in an extraordinary manner, having only two eyes but a double nose. The creature holds its prominent breasts in its human hands; its feet are cloven.

1, 2
Canterbury—beam supporters from a house

Another hermaphroditic creature from Canterbury (2), likewise carved in wood, has a hideous face with heavily wrinkled brow, staring eyes and a toothy grin. Again the feet are cloven, and the large, coarse hands grasp the full, female breasts above the bovine haunches. Another in wood from Canterbury represents a full-faced figure, with coarse features and deeply-drilled pupils which impart an intense staring quality to the eyes. The feet are cloven, the haunches bovine; the human hands press the emphatic breasts together behind a shield-like device which is

held in front of the creature. Bovine ears appear to emerge from the head to blend into the woodwork above the figure. Another from Canterbury, this time in stone (3), sits grimly in a corner and gazes down, with huge eyes staring out of a half animal, half demoniac face. The left hand supports the left cheek, the knees are turned inwards. The breasts of this very unfeminine creature are large and full. The whole is extremely grotesque and repulsive.

Another strange creature is carved in wood at the medieval Feathers Inn at Ludlow, Shropshire (4). A figure with a male head, bearded and

3 *Right*
Canterbury—a figure on the north wall
4 *Above*
Ludlow, Shropshire—decoration from the façade at The Feathers Inn

moustached, stands in an attitude reminiscent of a caryatid supporting a beam with his upraised arms. He appears to have male nipples as well as female breasts. Between his legs hangs a long strip of carved foliage. His toes grip a bar of wood in simian fashion above a pair of severed heads joined by a twisted, rope-like piece of wood. Both heads are very reminiscent of Celtic severed heads, which is not surprising in this district. The severed head had a fertility significance for the Celts. The whole of this composition has a voluptuous, sensuous look about it.

Mermaid and Merman

Among the unlikely pagan members of the Gothic ecclesiastical pantheon we must count the mermaid and merman. Although we do not know with what significance they were imbued by the people responsible for creating them, they were no doubt used to express a number of different concepts. Sometimes they are depicted in conjunction with dolphins; often the mermaid appears alone, with her mirror and comb symbols. Canterbury Cathedral, Kent, with its marvellous repertoire of roof bosses, has a charming mermaid (1). With bifurcated tail, she

1 *Left*
Canterbury—a roof boss in the cloisters

2 *Below*
Berchtesgaden, Germany—detail of pillar decoration in the cloisters

brandishes her mirror and comb and gazes down with an expression of tranquillity. From the cathedral at Sens, Yonne, France, comes a beguiling example of a mermaid (3). She grasps her elaborately-fashioned tail with her left hand; her graceful, backwards-looking posture, the seaweed which forms her hair, and the web-like fins or wings on either side of her body all impart the impression of lightness, and give to the figure a floating quality which is very charming.

A magnificent, very pagan-looking merman comes from Berchtesgaden, Germany (2). This splendid head is bearded and moustached and with lentoid eyes outlined with a double line. It has a neck, but no body; from

below the neck springs a double tail forming a frame for the face. The whole impression is majestic and remote. An attractive pair of little mermen form part of the decoration of Schaffhausen church, Switzerland (4). Flanking an inscription, their seaweed-like garments divide to reveal scaly tails. A swag under the tablet, similarly decorated, forms a pleasant link between the two cherub-like mermen. Also from Schaffhausen (5) comes a magnificent merman, bold and confident, who gazes imperiously upwards from beneath his thatch of undulating hair. His body is powerful, and his

3, 4 *Below and right*
Schaffhausen, Switzerland—
corbels
5 *Below right*
Sens, France—cornice decoration

great scaly tail is bifurcated and adorned with seaweed. He holds it proudly aloft, with either hand, and the serpent-like ends coil round his arms. Another example comes from Patrixbourne, Kent (6), in which two small, almost sphinx-like mermaids form part of the decoration, facing each other and separated by foliage. They rest on their stomachs, each with a claw-like arm raised, with grim faces and with sinuous single tails which curve round to end in broad seaweed-like motifs.

6 *Above*
Patrixbourne, Kent—archway
decoration detail

88

Serpents: St George Motif

Dragons, serpents, and the theme of
the perpetual fight against them by
man, saint or god, have always
received high popularity in the
Christian Church. A favourite theme
in pagan Celtic Europe was the
battle between the great rider god,
Taranis, 'The Thunderer', and the
reptilian monster, like a footed serpent; either he tramples this victor-
iously under the hooves of his steed,
or treads its head down into the

earth. St George and his legendary fight, and St Michael in a similar combat, represent ancient concepts of the spiritual warfare constantly engaged in by good against the ever-menacing forces of evil. There are many representations of this motif, and many dragon or serpentiform gargoyles and grotesques, in the repertoire of the Christian Church. Some hint at the theme, some give a more detailed account.

From Belgrade, Yugoslavia, comes an illustration of St George, with intrepid skill, spearing his vicious protagonist (1). A wood-carving at the Star Inn, Alfriston, Sussex (3), shows the same motif. The slender saint rushes courageously forward to pierce his monstrous opponent, with its forked tongue and toothy jaws. An interesting feature of this dragon is the tail in the form of the head and neck of a swan. From the same building comes a double serpent/dragon ornament (2). The two creatures are differently portrayed, each having a fierce animal head; the tongue of one

2, 3 *Above left and below left*
Alfriston, Sussex—details from the façade of the Star Inn
4 *Right*
Canterbury—a roof boss in the cloisters

beast protrudes menacingly. The tails are entwined, to make a single unit of the conjoined beasts.·

A rich roof boss in Canterbury Cathedral, Kent (4), is composed of human heads completely entwined by serpents. A water-spout at Westminster Abbey (7) is formed by the tongue, curled up at the edges, of a fierce creature with a semi-human head, a great open mouth, a huge clawed front leg and a body suggestive of a dragon or serpent. At Millstatt, Austria (*see* Column

5, 6 *Left and far left*
Millstatt, Austria—cornice
decorations
7 *Above*
Westminster Abbey—a gargoyle
on the east front

Figures), is a sinister dragon-like
beast, crawling down a column,
nostrils flaring, eyes staring, ears flat
back on its head (5). The foliate
motif before its grinning mouth gives
the impression of darts and flames
coming from its fearsome maw. Also
from Millstatt comes another dragonesque creature (6) in the same
attitude. It snarls its way down the
column, its great tongue folded and
ready to flick out at an unwary
passer-by. From the cathedral at
Troyes, Aube, France, the splendid
pair of dragon-like creatures (8)
comprises one in the form of a
winged lizard without hind legs and
another, also without hind legs, with

a baleful, cat-like head, a heavy body, front legs and a sinuous, serpent-like tail.

From Kilpeck, Herefordshire (*see* Kilpeck), comes a fine series of dragonesque and serpentiform shapes. One (9) shows the motif of four biting dragon or serpent heads, each biting the neck of the one in front. Another dragon-like creature from the same church (10) bites its own tail—a familiar motif—and is winged, with a single powerful claw. Yet another turns back, its mouth

8 *Left*
Troyes, France—exterior decoration
9, 10 *Above and below*
Kilpeck, Herefordshire—archway decorations on the west door

11 *Left*
Iffley, Oxfordshire—a roof boss
12 *Above*
Dover, Kent—carvings
surrounding a steeple

fiercely open, with a single-clawed foot visible, and a sharply-coiled tail. Some highly complex imagery at Iffley, Oxfordshire (11), comprises a great coiled dragon-like creature with four semi-human masks surrounding it. The mask to the right seems to be biting the monster's wing; while the monster seems to be seizing the head to the left with its clawed foot. Fruits and foliate motifs complete the picture. At Dover, Kent (12), is a group of great sinister monsters, crouching ready to spring, their fierce masks and intimidating attitude no doubt engaged in driving away from the fabric of the church all the evil which constantly beset it.

The Mallet God

One of the oldest and most widespread of the pagan Celtic deities was the powerful god Sucellos, 'The Good Striker', with his mallet, his patera or goblet of plenty, and often his dog attribute. He is widely known from Celtic Europe, and he was invoked in Britain in Roman times. There is a simple portrayal of him with his mallet and dish on the west wall of Copgrove church, Yorkshire; the stone upon which he appears is locally known as The Devil's Stone, a sure sign of his pagan associations. An enigmatic figure who may perhaps suggest some memory of the pagan god, with his beneficent character, comes from Codford St Mary, Wiltshire (1). On this tapering stone panel a strange scene is depicted. A male figure wearing a pleated garment strides forward, perhaps in an attitude of dancing. He brandishes aloft in his right hand a bough of fruits and foliage, which he regards with his head turned. In his left hand he grasps a mallet. The narrower sides of the stone are decorated with foliate motifs. One may perhaps envisage here some sort of dance in honour of vegetation rites in which the ritual of the sacred mallet of Sucellos, or some equivalent deity, was remembered. Sucellos was essentially a god of fertile provision and fecundity. His mate was the territorial goddess, with her horn of plenty and her power over the produce of the earth.

Left
Codford St Mary, Wiltshire—a carved stone pillar subsequently incorporated into an inside wall

Lunar and Solar Heads

In all religions the sun and the moon have their place in divine imagery, whatever the significance of their particular role. Portrayal of these heavenly bodies does not necessarily mean to say that they were worshipped for their own sake; but they were much used to embody the forces of divinity and to give them a tangible and familiar visual expression. The Christian Church has its full complement of such imagery. One of the most impressive, perhaps, is to be seen at Chartres Cathedral; here the two towers are each topped with gleaming weathercocks, one in the form of the sun, the other shaped like a crescent moon. Chartres Cathedral, like so many others, is built over a pagan Celtic shrine, and the atmosphere there is very marked and archaic. The site was that of the central annual meeting place of the Druids, the pagan Celtic priests, and something of its ancient sanctity lingers on, in conjunction with the Christian sacredness of the place.

From Millstatt, Austria (*see* Column Figures), comes this strange stone head (1), with deeply drilled eyeballs and nostrils, gazing out over the crescent moon. From the Feathers Inn, Ludlow, Shropshire, we have this very fine painted ceiling (2) in which the solemn, radiate sun looks down, connected with the fruit-bearing branches surrounding it which make up the rest of the decoration.

Centaurs

Amongst the numerous other pagan symbols taken into the repertoire of Christian iconography, to be used in a variety of ways, is the motif of the centaur, half-horse, half-man. A fine and somewhat sinister example (1) can be seen among the rich imagery at Millstatt, Austria (*see* Column Figures). Here a strange male face, bearded and unsmiling, forms the support of a horned centaur. Like those of the face, the centaur's eyeballs are deeply pierced, adding to the intensity of the expression. The figure, which is human to below the armpits, has arms, and brandishes what may be a mallet in its right hand. The left foreleg is raised and held in the left hand. The left hind leg, which appears to be hooved, is raised; the whole attitude is confident and severe. From Autun, Saône et Loire, France, come many pieces of impressive imagery, among them, in a roundel (2), a centaur turning his head and shoulders to shoot an arrow backwards from his bow at some unseen target. His radiate hair is stiff, his hooved legs short, his horse body elongated. He has a long tail like a lion's, with a tuft at the end, which, in lion-like fashion, curls between his legs up over his back.

A very strange scene concerned

3, 4, 5 *Above and below left and above right*
Iffley, Oxfordshire—capitals of the east doorway
6 *Below right*
Adel, Yorkshire—capital

with centaurs occurs at Iffley church, Oxfordshire (3). Here, a female centaur rears up on her hind legs and gives her left breast to a male centaur to suck. His hind legs are raised, his forelegs plunge forward in the direction of his nurturer, whilst round the corner of the column another centaur grasps his bow with his left hand and offers food with his right to the female centaur of the first illustration, presumably from a sheep, which he has apparently killed (4). At Iffley again, a man with animal hind-quarters seizes a griffin-like creature with his hands and seeks to tear its jaws open (5).

A mythological scene involving centaurs survives in Adel church, Yorkshire (6). Here a centaur, wearing a peaked helmet, brandishes his bow and arrow at a griffin-like creature having foliate decoration springing from its mouth. From

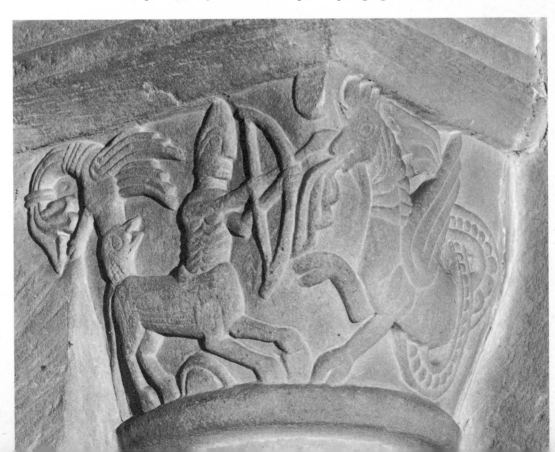

Trogir, Yugoslavia (8), we have a sturdy centaur grasping his draped coat in either hand. An animal crouches beside a tree, while below, a most interesting creature, horned and hoofed, with human features, beard and long hair, stands upright. He is covered with animal fur, like a wood-wose, and his hands, raised in the *orans* posture, are covered with foliage. This would seem to be a portrayal of the ancient European horned god, lord of the woodlands and wild things.

From Kilpeck (*see* Kilpeck) comes a half-sphinx, half-centaur (7), with human features but with mane, claws and tail, the tail in the position in which so many tails of conventional lions are portrayed—between the hind legs and coming up and over the back. This sinister creature stalks warily on the walls of this magnificent building.

7 *Above*
Kilpeck, Herefordshire—detail of the archway decoration
8 *Left*
Trogir, Yugoslavia—detail of main entrance decoration

Hagodays

The hagoday, the sanctuary knocker, comprises a large escutcheon of bronze decorated with the head of some monstrous beast which sometimes holds a human head in its jaws. Many hagodays date to the fourteenth century; an example dating to about 1140 is situated on the south door of Durham Cathedral. If the hunted person could reach the sanctuary knocker and lay hold of it, he was supposed to be protected by the church and his pursuers to be powerless to seize him. The fine example illustrated here is at Dubrovnik, Yugoslavia. It has all the features of true grotesque; tongue protruding, fierce mouth grasping the freedom-conveying ring, foliage crowning the frowning head with its stiff, radiate tufts of fur.

Column Figures

1 *Left*
Roquepertuse, Bouches-du-Rhône, France—the original door-frame of the Celto-Ligurian sanctuary, with actual human skulls set in niches
2, 3 *Above left and above right*
Millstadt, Austria—columns in the west doorway

The remarkable church at Millstatt, Austria, contains a splendid range of figures on its elaborately decorated columns, into which faces are apparently embedded. These carvings bear so great a resemblance to the third-century Celto-Ligurian sanctuary (1) from Roquepertuse in France as to defy coincidence.

In the Roquepertuse sanctuary actual human skulls are still to be found in niches in the square columns. Some of the niches are now empty but doubtless once also contained human heads or skulls; the

Millstatt carvings suggest the former to have been the case. Typical of the iconography of Millstatt is a head (2) with fleshy, naturalistic face framed by springing locks of hair and, emerging from the column above, foliage decoration. Another face (3) with similar but even more sinister appearance peers mask-like out through the spirals of the column, like a face from the folds of a shroud, the eyes staring sightlessly upwards, the nostrils wide and deeply cut, the lower part of the face completely swathed in the fold-like

convolutions of the column. Another elaborately-decorated column (4) from Dreieichen, Austria, has as its support the fine head of an aged man. His eyebrows emphasize the power of his full eyes with their deeply-defined pupils. His drooping moustaches blend with the long, elaborately-dressed beard.

One column is topped by two great eagle-like birds, their heads turned backwards and each with a powerful claw gripping the crown of an elongated severed head. It rises from a corbel decorated with an impressive male head (5), which resembles number 4 in general style, but differs in detail. The mouth droops more, ears are depicted, and the heavy, abundant beard is twisted into an elaborate pattern.

4, 5 *Above left and right* Dreieichen, Nr Hollabrunn, Austria—external column decorations

Sphinx

The sphinx is a widely popular motif of ancient eastern origin, which is usually composed of a human and lion, or other beast, having wings. In Egypt it represented the Sun God Harmackhis to whom the phoenix was the sacred bird. The lion body represented wisdom and power, the wings probably refer to the phoenix. One, from Schaffhausen, Switzerland (1), has close sculptural affinities with a merman from the same building (*see* Mermaid and Merman, 5). Here a powerful male head rises from a torso which merges into a bird body with swelling, upraised wings; the furred legs are seemingly those of a lion. The creature stands on a swag of foliage which nicely matches and balances the left wing.

Other sphinx-like creatures, both male and female, adorn capitals in the cathedral at Sens, Yonne,

2, 3 *Left and right*
Sens, France—capitals in the nave

France. These are depicted in a variety of attitudes, some frontal, others reversed but with heads turned back. One female example, having the body of an eagle-like bird and the forepaws of a lion (2), stands poised with raised wings. She is flanked by two male sphinxes, the bearded and moustached heads of which very much carry on the tradition of Gallo-Roman divine masks. These, too, have wings stretched as if for flight. Sophisticated foliate and roseate motifs separate the figures. On another capital a female creature has a reptile's tail, like that of a chameleon, a face naturalistically portrayed, like that of all these examples, and wings raised close together above the backwards-gazing head. She is separated by a foliate motif from a male composite creature, with fine head bearing crown or diadem, a similar reptilian tail, and two strong leonine legs. The wings are raised in a similar attitude to that adopted by those of the female.

Again, from the same building, we have another variant on this theme

110

(3). The foliate decoration here takes the form of two trees, divided into two main branching boughs which are skilfully linked with the two composite creatures which stand beside them. The female figure on the left, her long straight hair twined about the bough, looks towards her companion but not at him; her face has an enigmatic, semi-smiling expression. Like her fellow she has her wings folded along her sides. Leaves fall over her back. Her long, snake-like tail can just be discerned behind her powerful, cloven-hoofed leg. The second figure, a male, is also of youthful appearance. His short, stranded hair falls against the bough which spreads its foliage above him and over his folded wings. He too has a coiled, serpent-like tail; his powerful foot is clawed, like that of a predator or a lizard.

The sphinxes in medieval churches, whilst clearly derived from the east and presumably brought by the Romans, also incorporate other features more in line with the Celtic beliefs of their new surroundings.

Nobodies

A great corpus of mysterious creatures having a head, with limbs protruding from it, but no clearly-defined body, forms another strange item in the motley assortment of obscure motifs which combine to make up the imagery of the medieval church. A fine example (1) from Lowick, Northumberland, is typical

of the genre, the significance of which is hard to apprehend today. Here the great face with its smallish eyes, broad, coarse nose and thick, sensual mouth, the whole seemingly enfolded in some veil-like covering, has arms growing from the side of the crown, perhaps terminating in hooves. Another example of this

1 *Left*
Lowick, Northumberland—a carved capital
2 *Above*
Dorchester, Oxfordshire—detail from a carved capital

strange imagery is at Dorchester, Oxfordshire (2). Here a fleshy face, again apparently shrouded with some kind of veil, holds a severed male head grimly in thick, powerful fingers, while a heavy leg, apparently terminating in a clawed foot, emerges from the side of the head above the arm.

As with so many other grotesque representations, the Nobodies are to be found all over Europe. If our other Celtic analogies are to be maintained it would not be unreasonable to suppose that there would be a connection here between Celtic worship of the severed head and what could be seen as a sort of 'severed head spirit'.

113

Kilpeck

The church of St Mary and St David, Kilpeck, Herefordshire, is unique in English Romanesque. Dating from the twelfth century, it is adorned with a rich repertoire of imagery of every kind, which draws on a wide variety of sources for its inspiration, including the Anglo-Saxon and the ancient pagan themes of Celtic Britain. For this reason it is given a separate section here so that some of its richness may be appreciated and explored. The church is entered by the south doorway (1), where the fineness of the workmanship and the sophistication of the various carvings testify to the great artistic skill and masterly craftsmanship of the creators. The diverse symbolic objects are combined to produce a rare and harmonious whole. The decoration of the outermost order of the arch begins with fierce, fanged, wolf-like creatures, highly ornamented and elaborate (2). They glare upwards towards a sequence of medallions, linked by fierce masks, each one different and displaying varying degrees of humanness. The medallions contain creatures including birds of different kinds, serpents, or intertwined non-naturalistic beasts. The medial order displays a range of superbly carved motifs, pagan and Christian, including several fine beaked heads, a biting serpentiform monster, intertwined beasts and others. Beneath the dog-

toothed third order or the arch is the
tympanum, finely decorated with a
highly stylized tree. The tree, which
is presumably to be interpreted as the
Tree of Life, achieves a rare harmony
without symmetry, a characteristic of
Celtic art itself; some memory of this
style, or some actual experience of
Celtic art objects, may have inspired
the artist to depict the tree in this

manner.

The jambs of the doorway are
richly carved with striking and
unusual scenes. The western capital
is adorned with two dragon-like
beasts engaged in combat, the eastern by a splendid foliate mask from
either side of the mouth of which
vegetation sprouts boldly, taking up
the theme of the tree in the tym-

3, 4 *Left and right*
Kilpeck—details of west door jamb
decoration

116

panum. The outer shafts of the jambs are adorned with magnificent, elaborately coiled serpents, those on the west gazing downwards, those on the east, upwards. The inner shaft of the eastern jamb is decorated with a design of birds and scrollwork, gentle and pleasing. The inner shaft of the western jamb is totally different, yet the whole is harmonious. Two enigmatic figures are portrayed (3, 4). They wear ribbed shirts (or mail), long, loose trousers and knotted girdles, and on their heads Phrygian bonnets. Each appears to hold a weapon or implement.

The row of corbels which runs round the outside of the church beneath the eaves portrays a great variety of objects and motifs, many

117

heads among them. On the west wall, at either end and at the top of a central pilaster, the jaws of three monstrous creatures protrude boldly, the mouths filled with grotesque, serpent-like tongues, the eyes lentoid and malevolent (5). The west window is adorned with an elaborately decorated engaged arch with columns (6). The capitals are formed by Green Man heads, closely similar to that on the eastern capital of the south door (1). Foliage springs boldly from the gaping mouths; the severity of the features is emphasized by the thin, drooping moustaches and the heavy brows which shadow large, almond-shaped eyes.

On balance there is far more pagan decoration to the church than Christian and one can only wonder therefore to what degree the beliefs of its first congregations are reflected in the images with which they surrounded themselves.

5 *Above left*
Kilpeck—the west wall
6 *Right*
Kilpeck—the west window

Miscellaneous

Several gargoyles and grotesques in the foregoing classifications can be cross-referenced, owing to the fact that they contain features which would make them equally apposite to one or more related groups. There are also numerous examples which do not seem to fit comfortably into any of these classifications.

From Ewelme, Oxfordshire, comes an extraordinary figure with distorted, human body and monkey-like face (3). He squats, gripping his knees with powerful hands, and stares morosely out into the distance. He wears a buttoned, long-sleeved tunic on the powerful upper part of his body; the lower part is disproportionately represented, as are the short, stocky legs and feet. A scene of demons seemingly trying to pull away a cherub (2) comes from Sens, Yonne, France. The devil on the left has three fingers and a thumb on his right hand; he appears to be dragging the cherub in the direction of a foliate head which has a sinister, mask-like expression. The goblin to the right of the cherub faces it, and seems to be pulling it towards him with his right hand; his left hand rests on his flank. The garlanded, winged cherub presses his left leg against the wall as if to prevent himself from being dragged into the clutches of the left-hand demon, and gazes serenely upwards.

A wooden panel from Assisi, Umbria, Italy (1), would be apposite to several of our themes. Starting at the base of this complex and fine piece we see two griffin-like creatures

1 *Left*
Assisi, Italy—carved wooden door panel
2 *Above*
Sens, France—a corbel decoration

121

3 *Left*
Ewelme, Oxfordshire—a corbel
4 *Right*
Autun, France—a doorway
decoration
5 *Below right*
Doge's Palace, Venice—detail of
bronze fountain decoration

within medallions of foliage; above them is a glaring ram-horned monster with frowning brow, broad flat nose and long pointed beard above which the hideous gaping mouth reveals a fierce tongue. This mask is very similar to that which features on many of the hagodays, or sanctuary-knockers. A crest springs from the top of the head, rising to support a vase on which stands an aggressive eagle. On either side of this are creatures like winged horses with long, leonine tails swelling into foliate-motif canine heads. Two small, winged serpents confront each other angrily on the vase, their tails running into rosettes; on either side of them dance savage satyrs, bearing goat-horns and holding long strings of bead-like decoration in their upraised hands. In this complex imagery on a single

panel we find many motifs which are echoed singly throughout the medieval world.

From Venice, Italy, comes a superb Silenus-like figure (5). His intimidating face leers down towards his naked torso which terminates in a Gorgon-type mask. All about him are festooned fruits and foliage, which two lush, reclining figures sample or survey. In the background is a frieze of vases and rosettes. While, from Autun, Saône et Loire, France, come two roundels of stone separated by stylized trees (4). The one on the left represents some domestic activity, perhaps grape-pressing; the lizard-like creature on the right, huge in proportion to the man, holds some circular object under its left fore-foot, and its small eyes peer out with watchful intensity.

In the entrance to the Cathedral of Lisbon in Portugal there are the usual series of decorative columns with carved capitals. One of these (6) depicts what seems to be a battle between two mounted riders, the warriors are waving weapons, a sword and a club, and have their arms extended wildly. There is nothing strange about them, it is their mounts which are so curious. On the right, the animal has a rear paw visible which is certainly no horse's hoof, there is a long cat-like tail and the head could be that of a bear or possibly a lioness. Its front leg is raised but it grips the horn of the opposing beast with a human hand.

The animal on the left has few distinguishing features and could be

some sort of horse except for the fact that it has a single horn projecting from the left side of its head. This horn is plainly of great importance since it is in the centre of the group, and both of the warriors as well as the other beast all have a hand stretched out to it.

Could this be a representation of the mythical battle of the Lion and the Unicorn? If so, who are the two warriors? What indeed is the significance of this scene?

One thing we hope has been established in the course of this book: the medieval artists were not engaged in haphazard decoration merely for decoration's sake; everything they did had a purpose and it is not their fault that we do not really know much about it. It seems more than likely that in the centuries which have passed since the work was done, the establishment of the church has seen to it that we forget what those grotesque carvings are for. However, as a great deal of the grotesque art has happily survived we can perhaps start to piece it together again. Almost every answer starts new questions but the pieces of this manuscript are so many and spread so wide that the possibilities for finding solutions are as great as our patience in searching.

6 Lisbon Cathedral, Portugal—capital of a column in the main entrance.

Select Bibliography

Anderson, M. D. *History and Imagery in British Churches* (1971), with good bibliography
Cave, C. J. P. *Roof Bosses in Medieval Churches* (1948)
Pevsner, N. County volumes in 'Buildings of England' series, Penguin Books
Ross, Anne *Pagan Celtic Britain* (1967)
Royal Commissions on Ancient and Historic Monuments; the *Inventories*,
Victoria History of the Counties of England series, for descriptions of individual churches

Other books by the authors include:
Anne Ross *Pagan Celtic Britain, Everyday Life of the Pagan Celts*
Ronald Sheridan (as photographer) *Jerusalem—Sacred City, Quest for Theseus,
Art Treasures of Eastern Europe, House of David, Crucible of Christianity*

Index